Nita Mehta's
MUGHLAI
Vegetarian Khaana

Enjoy the rich Mughlai taste and aroma!

Nita Mehta

B.Sc. (Home Science), M.Sc. (Food and Nutrition), Gold Medalist

SNAB
Publishers Pvt Ltd

D0544592

Nita Mehta's
MUGHLAI
Vegetarian Khaana

8th Reprint 2002
ISBN 81-86004-10-6

Food Styling and Photography: **SNAB**

Layout and laser typesetting :

 National Information Technology Academy
3A/3, Asaf Ali Road, New Delhi-110002
☎ 3252948

Published by :

SNAB Publishers Pvt. Ltd.
3A/3 Asaf Ali Road, New Delhi - 110002
Tel: 3252948, 3250091
Telefax:91-11-3250091

Editorial and Marketing office:
E-348, Greater Kailash-II, N.Delhi-48
*Fax:*91-11-6235218 *Tel:*91-11-6214011, 6238727
E-Mail: nitamehta@email.com
snab@snabindia.com
*Website:*http://www.nitamehta.com
Website: http://www.snabindia.com

Distributed by :

THE VARIETY BOOK DEPOT
A.V.G. Bhavan, M 3 Con Circus,
New Delhi - 110 001
Tel : 3327175, 3322567; Fax : 3714335

Printed by :

THOMSON PRESS (INDIA) LIMITED

Rs. 89/-

With love to my family members
&
TO ALL
who wish to be recognized and appreciated as
good Cooks !

ALL ABOUT MUGHLAI KHAANA

Mughlai food is the food that was eaten and relished by the Indians during the Mughal period. Mughlai khaana stands apart as the empress of the Indian range of cooking. It lays stress on good ingredients, low flame and rich spices. Ingredients such as badaam (almonds), khus khus (poppy seeds) and flavouring spices such as illaichi (cardamom), dalchini (cinnamon), laung (cloves), javitri (mace) and jaiphal (nutmeg) are used to prepare Mughlai food. Curd and cream form the gravies having less stress on tomatoes. Onions are usually deep fried to a golden brown colour and then blended to a paste and used in gravies.

Kebabs are the speciality of Mughlai cooking and served as snacks as well as meal time accompaniments. Rice preparations, such as "Biryani", holds a special place in Mughlai food.

A special way of decorating both savoury and sweet Mughlai dishes is to use 'Varq' - beaten silver leaf, which is edible.

Nita Mehta

CONTENTS

Gulbahaar-E-Subz

ZAFRANI KOFTA

Picture on page 17
Serves 6

KOFTAS
150 gms paneer (cottage cheese) - grated
2 small boiled potatoes - grated
2 slices of bread
½ tsp garam masala (mixed spices)
½ tsp red chilli powder, salt to taste
2-3 tbsp maida (plain flour) - to coat

FILLING
1 onion - very finely chopped
½ " piece ginger - very finely chopped
4-5 kaju - chopped
10-12 kishmish
¼ tsp each of salt, red chilli pd., garam masala

GRAVY

few strands kesar (saffron)
2 big onions, 1" piece ginger
1 dry red chilli
2 tej patta(bay leaf)
2-3 chhoti illaichi (green cardamom)
2 tbsp kaju (cashewnuts) - powdered
½ cup fresh curd - beaten with a fork
2 tbsp desi ghee
½ tsp garam masala, ½ tsp red chilli powder
1 tsp salt or to taste
½ cup fresh cream
½ cup milk mixed with ½ cup water

1. To prepare the koftas, mix grated paneer, potatoes, red chilli powder, salt & garam masala.
2. Cut sides of bread. Dip in water. Squeeze well. Add to the potato-paneer mixture. Mash well till smooth. Make 8-10 balls.
3. For the filling, heat 2 tsp ghee. Add onions & ginger & fry till golden

brown. Add kaju, salt, garam masala & chilli pd. Remove from fire.

4. Flatten each ball of paneer mixture, put 1 tsp of onion filling and one kishmish in each ball. Form a ball again. Roll each ball in maida.
5. Deep fry 2-3 koftas at a time in hot oil. Keep aside.
6. To prepare the gravy, soak kesar in 1 tbsp warm water.
7. Grind onions, ginger & dry red chilli to a fine paste. Heat 2 tbsp ghee in a heavy bottomed karahi & add the onion paste. Add tej patta & chhoti illaichi. Cook on low flame till onions turn transparent & ghee separates. Do not let the onions turn brown.
8. Add curd. Cook for 5-7 minutes till masala turns brown again.
9. Add kaju powder. Cook for 2-3 minutes. Add garam masala, red chilli powder & salt. Cook for ½ minute.
10. Add milk mixed with water, to make a gravy. Boil. Simmer on low flame for 5 minutes. Add kesar, keeping aside a little for garnishing.
11. Add fresh cream. Mix well. Add a pinch of sugar if the curd added was a little sour. Remove from fire.
12. To serve, boil gravy. Add koftas. Keep on low heat for ½ a minute. Serve immediately, sprinkled with cream & dotted with soaked kesar.

SUBZ SHAHJAHANI

Picture on 72
Serves 4

½ of a small cauliflower - deep fried
½ cup boiled or frozen peas
2 small carrots
10 15 french beans

SHAHJAHANI PASTE
1 tbsp khus khus (poppy seeds)
2 chhoti illaichi (green cardamom) - crushed
2" piece dry coconut - grated
OR
1tbsp dessicated coconut (nariyal ka burada)
2 laung (cloves)
1 tej patta (bay leaf)
1 flower javitri (mace)

13

MASALA

3 medium onions
1" piece ginger
1 cup curd - fresh
1 tsp salt or to taste
½ tsp red chilli pd.
½ tsp garam masala
½ cup milk
5 tbsp desi ghee

1. Scrape carrots and thread french beans. Chop carrots into ½" cubes and cut french beans diagonally into ½" (slanting) pieces. Cut cauliflower into small florets and deep fry to a golden brown colour.
2. Heat 2 tbsp ghee. Add beans & carrots. Cover & cook on low flame till done. Add ¼ tsp salt & garam masala.
3. To prepare the Shahjahani paste, heat ½ tbsp ghee in a heavy bottomed kadhai. Add khus khus, chhoti illaichi, dry coconut, laung, tej patta & javitri. Fry for 1 minute on a low flame, till the spices turn golden brown.

4. Remove tej patta. Grind the fried spices to a very fine paste. Keep the Shahjahani paste aside.
5. Grind 3 onions & ginger to a paste in a blender.
6. Heat 2½ tbsp ghee in a clean kadhai. Add the onion paste & cook till golden brown.
7. Reduce flame and add red chilli pd. Cook on low flame for 1-2 minutes more, till the onions turn brown and ghee separates.
8. Beat fresh curd with a fork till smooth and add it gradually to the onion masala. Cook stirring continuously till masala turns brown again & the masala becomes thick.
9. Add cooked peas, carrots & beans. Add salt to taste. Fry them in masala for 5 minutes. Add fried cauliflower.
10. Add 1 cup hot water & ½ cup milk. Boil.
11. Add the Shahjahani paste made with whole spices.
12. Cook, covered, for a few minutes till the vegetables are properly cooked & the masala coats the vegetables. Add a pinch of sugar if the curd added was a little sour. Remove from fire. Serve.

DILRUBA ALOO MATAR

Picture on page 35

Serves 4

4-5 small sized potatoes
2 tsp til (sesame seeds)
4 tbsp oil
½ tsp jeera (cumin seeds)
2 onions - cut into rings
1 tomato - pureed or 2 tbsp ready made tomato puree
8-10 kajus
10-15 kishmish - soaked in water for 10 minutes and drained
1 cup boiled or frozen peas
¾ tsp salt
½ tsp haldi
½ tsp garam masala, ½ tsp red chilli powder, ¼ tsp amchoor
2 tbsp chopped coriander
2 green chillies - slit lengthways

Zafrani Kofta : page 10

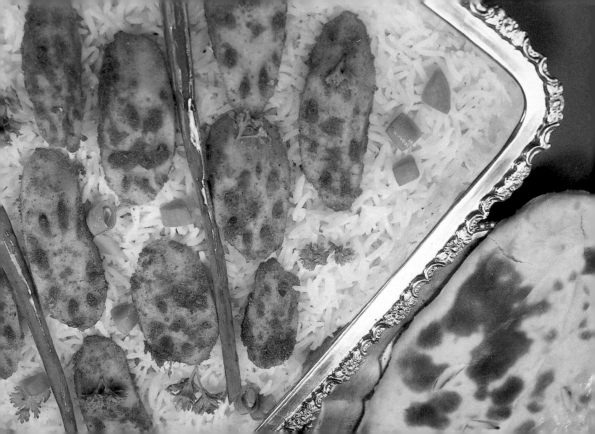

1. Boil potatoes in salted water until just tender and feel soft when a knife is inserted. Do not over cook. Peel. Cut each potato into 2 halves.
2. Dry-roast til on a tawa on low flame, until golden brown. Keep aside.
3. Heat oil. Add jeera. When it splutters and turns golden, add onions. Cook until onions turn golden.
4. Add kaju. Stir-fry till golden. Add tomato puree and cook till dry.
5. Add salt, garam masala, red chilli powder, amchoor, haldi, green chillies and fresh coriander. Cook for 1 minute.
6. Add the potatoes. Bhuno gently for about 5 minutes, taking care not to stir too often as this might break the potatoes. While bhunoing the potatoes, keep them spaced out and not overlapping each other so that they turn crisp.
7. Sprinkle til, keeping aside some for garnishing. Mix gently so that the potatoes are well coated with the til seeds.
8. Add boiled peas and kishmish. Stir to mix well. Remove from fire.
9. Transfer to a serving dish. Sprinkle some more til on the aloos. Serve.

Peshawari Bhein : page 66
Nan Badaami : page 112

19

SHAHI BABY CORNS

If baby corns are not available, regular corn on the cob can be used instead.

Picture on back cover

Serves 6

200 gm baby corns or 2 small tender bhutte (corn on the cobs)
2 cups milk
2 tbsp cashews - soaked for 10 minutes and ground to a paste with ¼ cup water

MASALA

3 small onions, 3 tomatoes, 1" piece ginger, 1 green chilli
4 tbsp oil, ½ tsp shah jeera
1 tsp dhania (coriander) powder, ½ tsp amchoor, 1½ tsp salt
¼ tsp haldi (turmeric) powder, ½ tsp red chili powder, 1 tsp garam masala
1 tsp tandoori masala, 2-3 chhoti illaichi (green cardamom) - seeds crushed
50 -100 gms paneer - grated (½-1 cup), 2 tbsp chopped coriander

BAGHAR OR TEMPERING

1 tbsp oil, ½ tsp shah jeera (black cumin), 1 tsp finely chopped ginger
5-6 almonds (badaam) - cut into thin long pieces, ¼ tsp red chilli powder

1. Choose small baby corns or thin tender bhuttas. Keep baby corns whole or cut each bhutta into 4 small pieces. If thick, slit each piece into two. Put all the pieces of baby corns and 2 cups milk in a pan. Add a pinch of haldi. Give one boil and keep on low heat for 2 minutes. If using bhuttas, pressure cook bhutta pieces with 2 cups milk to give one whistle. Then keep on low flame for 5 minutes. Remove from fire.
2. Blend onions, tomatoes, green chilli and ginger to a paste in a grinder.
3. Heat oil. Add shah jeera. After a minute, add onion-tomato paste and cook till dry and oil separates. Reduce flame. Add red chilli pd, haldi, dhania, amchoor, salt and garam masala. Cook for 1 minute.
4. Add cashew paste. Stir to mix well.
5. Keeping the flame low, add the left over milk from the boiled bhuttas, stirring continuously. Stir for 2-3 minutes.
6. Add corn and simmer on low flame for 3 minutes. Add enough (2-3 cups) water to get a thin gravy. Boil. Simmer for 5-7 minutes till slightly thick. Add tandoori masala, chhoti illaichi, paneer & coriander.
7. To serve, put the hot vegetable in the serving dish. Heat oil for tempering. Add jeera and ginger. After a few seconds, add almonds. Add red chilli pd, remove from fire. Pour oil on the gravy.

MATAR MASALA
Serves 4

1½ cups frozen peas (Safal or Green Valley)
1 potato - cut into big cubes
3 onions - finely chopped
½ tsp jeera (cumin seeds)
½ " piece ginger - chopped finely
2 green chilli - finely chopped
2 tomatoes - finely chopped
1½ tsp tandoori masala
½ tsp salt or to taste
½ tsp garam masala
4 tbsp oil

1. Deep fry big cubes of potato on low flame so that they get cooked on frying. Keep fried potatoes aside.
2. Heat oil. Add jeera. When it splutters, add onion. Cook till onions turn light brown.
3. Add ginger & green chilli. Cook for 1 minute.
4. Add tomatoes. Cook for 5-7 minutes till oil separates.
5. Add 3-4 tbsp water. Boil.
6. Add the peas. Add salt, tandoori masala & garam masala.
7. Cook, covered on low flame, stirring occasionally till peas are done.
8. At serving time, sprinkle a little water in the vegetable. Heat well.
9. Reduce flame and mix in the fried potatoes. Heat for a few seconds more. Serve hot.

MUGHLAI DUM ALOO

Picture on page 54
Serves 4

5 (250 gm) small sized potatoes
3 onions - sliced finely
3 tbsp magaz (watermelon seeds)
1 tbsp khus khus (poppy seeds)
3 small tomatoes - chopped roughly
1" piece ginger - chopped
½ tsp jeera (cumin seeds)
½ tsp red chilli pd.
½ tsp garam masala
¼ tsp amchoor
1¼ tsp salt or to taste
3 tbsp oil

1. Peel and cut potatoes into two equal halves. Deep fry on medium flame till golden brown. Remove from oil and keep aside.
2. Deep fry sliced onions to a golden brown colour. Remove from oil and grind the fried onions to a paste with a little water if required. Keep onion paste aside.
3. Soak magaz and khus khus together in 2-3 tbsp water for 15 minutes. Grind to a fine paste.
4. Boil tomatoes, ginger & ½ cup water together in a pan. Cover and cook till water dries up & the tomatoes turn soft. Grind to a paste.
5. Heat 3 tbsp oil. Add jeera. When it splutters, add red chilli powder.
6. Add the onion paste. Cook for 2 minutes on low flame.
7. Add the tomato paste. Cook for 4-5 minutes on low flame till oil separates.
8. Add magaz paste, salt, garam masala & amchoor. Stir for 2 minutes.
9. Add 1 cup water. Boil. Add fried potatoes. Simmer on low heat for 5-7 minutes till potatoes are well cooked and coated with masala.
10. Serve hot garnished with chopped coriander and magaz.

DAL MAKHANI

Picture on page 35

Serves 6

1 cup urad saboot (whole black beans)
2 tbsp channe ki dal (split gram dal)
2 tbsp rajmah (kidney beans) - soaked for 5-6 hours (optional)
4 tbsp ghee or oil
5 cups of water
1½ tsp salt, or to taste
1" piece ginger, 4 flakes garlic (optional)
2 dry red chillies
4 tomatoes - pureed in a grinder
½ cup cream
2 tsp dhania (coriander) powder, ½ tsp garam masala (mixed spices)
¼ tsp grated jaiphal (nutmeg)
2 tbsp butter
2 tsp kasoori methi (dry fenugreek leaves)

1. Grind ginger, garlic & dry red chillies together to a paste.
2. Clean, wash dals. Pressure cook both dals and the soaked rajmah with 1 tbsp ghee, water, salt and half of the ginger-garlic paste. Keep the left over paste aside.
3. After the first whistle, keep on low flame for 40 minutes. Remove from fire. Keep aside.
4. Heat 3 tbsp ghee. Add tomatoes pureed in a grinder. Cook until ghee separates and it turns thick.
5. Add the left over ginger paste, garam masala & coriander powder. Cook for a few seconds. Add this tomato mixture to the boiled dal.
6. Add butter and kasoori methi. Simmer on low flame for 15 minutes.
7. Add cream and jaiphal. Mix. Remove from fire.
8. Garnish with a bunch of uncut coriander leaves dipped in chilled water for 15 minutes. Arrange the leaves in the centre of the dish & make thin white rings of thick cream or well beaten curd around the coriander, pouring it with a small spoon. Serve hot.

BHINDI-DO PYAZA
Serves 4

½ kg bhindi (lady's finger) - small & tender
2 onions - sliced finely
150 gms baby onions
6 tbsp oil

POWDERED MASALA
1½ tsp salt
1 tsp red chilli pd.
4 tsp dhania (coriander) powder
1 tsp garam masala (mixed spices)
1 tsp haldi (turmeric pd.)
2 tsp amchoor (dried mango pd.)

OTHER INGREDIENTS
1 tsp saunf (aniseeds)

1 tsp jeera (cumin seeds)
1 tsp saboot dhania (coriander seeds)

1. Wash, dry lady's finger.
2. Slice off ¼" from the top & the bottom of each lady's finger. Slit them lengthways.
3. Mix all ingredients of the powdered masala together.
4. Peel baby onions & give 2 cuts (slits) crossing each other on the top, leaving the bottom part intact .
5. Fill the whole onions & lady's fingers with the powdered masala.
6. Heat oil. Add sliced onions. Cook till light brown. Add whole onions & lady's finger. Mix well.
7. Cook uncovered for 3-4 minutes.
8. Cover & cook for 4-5 minutes till half done.
9. Remove the cover and cook till it is crisp and completely cooked.
10. Crush saunf, jeera & saboot dhania to a powder and add to the lady's fingers. Cook for a few seconds. Serve hot.

TANDOORI PANEER
Serves 4

250 gms paneer - cut into 1" cubes
1½ " piece ginger
2-3 green chillies
1 tsp jeera (cumin seeds)
3-4 flakes garlic - optional
3/4 tsp salt
¼ tsp red chilli powder
a few drops orange red colour
1 tsp lemon juice
2 capsicums - cut into fine rings
2 onions - cut into fine rings
2 tbsp oil
2 tsp tandoori masala

1. Grind garlic, ginger, jeera & green chillies to a fine paste.
2. Add salt, chilli powder and lemon juice to the paste. Add enough orange colour to the paste.
3. Cut paneer into 1" squares. Apply 3/4 of this paste nicely on all the pieces. Keep the left over paste aside.
4. At the time of serving, keep this paneer in a greased dish and grill for 10 minutes till it is dry and slightly crisp. Alternately, paneer can be left like this (marinated) for 1 hour till dry.
5. Heat 2 tbsp oil in a kadhai. Fry onion & capsicum rings for a few minutes till onions turn transparent.
6. Add the left over ginger-garlic paste and few drops of lemon juice. Add ½ tsp salt.
7. Add paneer pieces. Sprinkle tandoori masala. Toss for a minute.
8. Serve immediately.

KHOYA MATAR MAKHAANA
Serves 4

1 cup shelled peas
100 gms khoya (dried whole milk)
1 cup makhaanas (puffed lotus seeds)
3 tomatoes - pureed
2 big onions
1" piece ginger
2 green chillies
1 tbsp chopped coriander
1 tbsp khus khus (poppy seeds)
1 tsp dhania (coriander pd.)
½ tsp red chilli pd.
½ tsp garam masala (mixed spices)
salt to taste
1 tbsp kishmish (raisins)

1. Fry makhaanas to a golden brown colour.
2. Grind onions, ginger, chillies & coriander leaves with a little water in a grinder.
3. Soak khus khus for 10-15 minutes & grind to a smooth paste.
4. Heat 4 tbsp oil. Add the onion-ginger paste. Cook on low heat till oil separates.
5. Add the khus khus paste. Cook for 1-2 minutes.
6. Add tomatoes pureed in a grinder. Cook till oil separates.
7. Add dhania pd, red chilli pd. and garam masala.
8. Grate khoya. Add khoya & mix well for 1 minute.
9. Add peas and makhaanas. Mix well.
10. Add kishmish.
11. Add enough water to get a thick gravy.
12. Cook covered till peas and makhaanas are done.
13. Serve hot, garnished with grated khoya.

GOBI GULISTAN

Picture on page 36
Serves 6

2 very small whole cauliflowers
4 tbsp oil

MASALA
3 onions - sliced finely
3 tomatoes - roughly chopped
1" piece ginger - chopped
2 tbsp curd
½ tsp garam masala
½ tsp red chilli powder
½ tsp amchoor
salt to taste
¼ cup boiled peas - to garnish

Dilruba Aloo Matar : page 16, Dal Makhani : page 26

1. Remove stem of cauliflower. Wash whole cauliflowers. Wipe dry with a clean towel.
2. Heat 5-6 tbsp oil in a kadhai. Put one cauliflower with flower side in oil. Cover & cook on medium flame, stirring occasionally till the cauliflower turns golden and gets cooked. Remove from oil. Fry the second cauliflower also & keep aside.
3. To prepare masala, grind onions to a paste.
4. Heat ½ tbsp oil in a clean kadhai. Add the chopped tomatoes & ginger. Cook for 4-5 minutes till they turn soft. Grind the cooked tomatoes to a paste.
5. Heat 3 tbsp oil in a kadahi. Add the onion paste, cook till onions turn brown.
6. Add cooked tomato paste. Cook for 3-4 minutes on low flame till masala turns dry.
7. Add well beaten curd. Cook till masala turns reddish again.

Gobi Gulistan : page 34

8. Add red chilli pd., amchoor & garam masala. Add salt to taste. Cook for 1 minute.
9. Add 2-3 tbsp water to get a thick, dry masala. Boil. Cook for 1 minute on low flame. Remove from fire.
10. Insert a little masala in between the florets of the fried cauliflower.
11. To serve, arrange the cauliflowers on a platter. Add 3-4 tbsp water to the masala to make it a little thin. Boil. Pour over the arranged cauliflowers. Heat in a preheated oven.

OR

Heat the cauliflower in a kadhai in 1 tbsp oil. Heat the masala separately by adding 2-3 tbsp water. Arrange the heated cauliflower on a serving platter. Pour the masala over it.
12. Sprinkle some boiled peas on it & on the sides. Serve.

HYDERABADI BAINGAN
Serves 4

250 gms small baingan (5-6 pieces)
6-7 tbsp oil

FILLING
2 tbsp til (sesame seeds)
a small piece fresh coconut - finely grated (3 -4 tbsp)
½ tsp salt
½ tsp red chilli powder
½ tsp amchoor pd.
¼ tsp sugar

MASALA
2 onions
1" piece ginger
2 dry, whole, red chillies

3 tomatoes
1 tsp dhania pd.
½ tsp amchoor (dried mango pd.)
1 tsp salt or to taste
½ tsp garam masala
2 pinches sugar

1. Wash baingans. Make two cross cuts from the top, leaving the end part intact.
2. Mix all ingredients of the filling together.
3. Fill 2 tsp filing in each baingan.
4. Heat 6-7 tbsp oil. Put the baingans in, and cook for 3-4 minutes stirring occasionally. Cover & cook for another 15 minutes till soft. Gently keep turning the baingans occasionally till very soft. Remove excess oil from kadhai & keep aside.
5. To prepare the masala, grind onions, ginger, red chillies & tomatoes together to a paste.

6. Heat 4 tbsp oil in a clean kadhai. Add the onion - tomato paste. Cook till almost dry.
7. Add dhania powder, amchoor, garam masala and salt. Cook on low flame till oil separates.
8. Add 1½ cups hot water to get a gravy. Simmer gravy for 5-7 minutes on low flame. Keep aside.
9. To serve, heat baingans separately. Sprinkle 2 pinches sugar, ¼ tsp amchoor & ¼ tsp salt on the baingans.
10. Heat the gravy separately.
11. Pour the gravy in a low sided dish. Carefully pick up each hot baingan and arrange neatly over the gravy.
12. Put a few drops of cream or well beaten curd on the gravy (not on the baingans) & arrange few boiled peas over the drops of cream. Serve.

KADHAI MUSHROOMS

Picture on page 53
Serves 4

200 gm (1 packet) fresh mushrooms - small sized
1 capsicum - cut into 1" pieces
2 onions - finely chopped
½ " piece ginger
5-6 flakes garlic
3 tomatoes - chopped finely
2 dry red chillies
1 tbsp saboot dhania (coriander seeds)
a pinch of methi dana (fenugreek seeds)
1 tsp salt or to taste
1 small tomato - cut into two halves - to garnish
2 green chillies - cut into thin long strips
5 tbsp oil

1. Grind ginger & garlic to a paste.
2. Powder together red chillies & saboot dhania on a chakla-belan.
3. Wash mushrooms well in plenty of water to remove any dirt.
4. If mushrooms are small, keep them whole, if big, cut into halves.
5. Cut 1 tomato into two big pieces for garnishing & keep aside. Chop the other 3 tomatoes finely.
6. Heat 5 tbsp oil. Add mushrooms. Cook covered, stirring occasionally, for 10 minutes till done.
7. Add capsicum. Cook on medium flame for 3-4 minutes. Remove mushroom & capsicum from oil.
8. In the same oil, and chopped onions & make them light brown.
9. Add ginger-garlic paste. Cook for ½ minute. Add dhania-chilli pd.
10. Add chopped tomatoes. Cook for 7-8 minutes, till oil separates.
11. Add methi dana & salt. Cook for ½ minute. Add ¼ cup water.
12. Add cooked mushrooms and capsicum. Stir-fry for 2-3 minutes.
13. Remove from fire. To garnish, heat 1 tbsp oil on a tawa. Add the tomato halves & slit green chillies. Saute for ½ minute. Garnish with glazed tomato halves & slit green chillies.

SHAHI KHOYA MATAR
Serves 4

150 gms khoya (dried whole milk)
1½ cups boiled peas
½ " piece ginger
2 green chillies
½ tsp jeera (cumin seeds)
a few cashewnuts
2 onions
2 tomatoes - pureed
1 tsp salt
¼ tsp red chilli powder
¼ tsp garam masala (mixed spices)
1 cup water
2 tbsp ghee

1. Grind green chillies, ginger and jeera to a fine paste.
2. Grind onions separately.
3. Heat ghee. Add onions. Cook until onions turn light brown.
4. Add mashed khoya. Cook on slow fire until khoya turns light brown.
5. Add ginger paste. Cook for 1 minute.
6. Add cashewnuts. Cook for ½ minute.
7. Add tomato puree. Cook until dry and well fried.
8. Add peas, keeping aside a few for garnishing. Stir for 2-3 minutes.
9. Add water, salt, red chillies and garam masala. Boil.
10. Cook on low flame, till the gravy turns thick.
11. Serve hot, garnished with grated khoya, cashewnuts and boiled peas.

METHI MALAI KHUMB MATAR

Picture on cover
Serves 4-5

200 gms mushrooms - preferably small in size
1 cup shelled, boiled or frozen peas
4 tbsp kasoori methi (dry fenugreek leaves)
1 tsp ginger-garlic paste
1 tbsp butter, 3 tbsp oil
2 onions - ground to a paste
¼ cup malai (milk topping) - mix with ¼ cup milk and blend in a mixer for a few
seconds till smooth or ½ cup thin fresh cream
1 tsp salt, or to taste, ½ tsp red chilli pd, ½ tsp garam masala, a pinch amchoor
1 cup milk (approx.)

GRIND TOGETHER
½ stick dalchini (cinnamon)
seeds of 2-3 chhoti illaichi (green cardamom), 3-4 laung (cloves)
4-5 saboot kali mirch (peppercorns), 2 tbsp cashewnuts

1. Trim the stem of each mushroom. Leave them whole if small or cut them into 2 pieces, if big. Heat 1 tbsp butter in a kadhai and add the mushrooms. Stir fry on high flame till dry and golden. Add 1 tsp ginger-garlic paste, ½ tsp salt and a pinch of white or black pepper. Stir for 1 more minute and remove from fire. Keep cooked mushrooms aside.
2. Grind together dalchini, seeds of chhoti illaichi, laung, kali mirch and cashews to a powder in a small mixer grinder.
3. Heat 3 tbsp oil. Add onion paste and cook on low heat till oil separates. Do not let the onions turn brown.
4. Add the freshly ground masala-cashew powder. Cook for a few seconds.
5. Add the kasoori methi and malai, cook on low heat for 2-3 minutes till malai dries up.
6. Add salt, red chilli pd, garam masala and amchoor. Stir for 1 minute.
7. Add the boiled peas and mushrooms.
8. Add 1 cup milk to get a thick gravy. Add ¼ cup water if the gravy appears too thick. Boil for 2-3 minutes. Serve.

KARELA MUSSALAM
Serves 6

½ kg karelas (bitter gourd) with stalks
3 onions - chopped finely
½ tsp red chilli pd.
½ tsp garam masala (mixed spices)
1½ tsp dhania (coriander) pd.
1½ tsp amchoor (dried mango powder)
¼ tsp salt
½ tsp saunf (aniseeds)
6-7 tbsp oil
4-5 baby onions
OR
2 onions - sliced finely

1. Peel karelas, keeping the stalks intact. Slit lengthways. Rub salt inside and on the surface of karelas. If there are big, hard seeds, remove them. Keep aside for 2-3 hours atleast or even more.
2. Fry chopped onions in 1½ tbsp oil till light brown. Add saunf, amchoor & dhania powder.
3. Add red chilli pd. and garam masala & ¼ tsp salt. Cook for 2-3 minutes. Remove from fire. Keep filling aside.
4. Wash karelas a few times to remove bitterness. Squeeze well. Deep fry karelas on medium flame till light brown. Remove from oil. Cool.
5. Fill with onions stuffing. Tie a thread over the karelas.
6. Heat 1 tbsp oil in a karahi. Add sliced or baby onions (slit halfway crosswise) in oil for a few minutes till golden brown.
7. Add the karelas. Cook covered, on slow fire for 8-10 minutes, stirring occasionally till they turn brown. Serve.

Note : If you want to prepare the karelas in the evening, peel and rub salt in the morning & keep covered in the fridge till the evening. They will not be bitter at all.

PAALAK KA SAALAN
Serves 6

½ cup channe ki dal (split gram)
½ kg paalak (spinach)
2 tomatoes - chopped finely
1-2 green chillies - chopped
½ " ginger - chopped
6-7 flakes garlic - optional
1 tsp dhania (coriander) powder
½ tsp garam masala (mixed spices)
½ tsp red chilli pd.
3 tbsp oil
1 onion - chopped

BAGHAR
2 tbsp desi ghee
2 dry red chillies
¼ tsp red chilli powder

1. Soak dal for ½ hour.
2. Wash, chop paalak leaves. Discard the stems. Chop finely.
3. Heat oil in a pressure cooker. Fry onions till golden brown.
4. Strain the soaked dal. Add dal, paalak, tomatoes, green chillies, ginger, garlic, dhania powder, garam masala and red chilli powder.
5. Add ¼ cup water.
6. Pressure cook to give 2 whistles, then cook on low heat for 8-10 minutes.
7. After the pressure comes down, mash the dal slightly.
8. To serve, heat & put the saalan in the serving dish.
9. For the baghaar, heat ghee in a small heavy bottomed pan. Shut off the fire. Add red chilli powder & dry red chillies. After 4-5 seconds, pour the ghee over the saalan in the dish. Mix lightly.
10. Serve immediately with boiled rice or chappatis.

VEGETABLE AKBARI
Serves 4

2 onions - cut into rings
½ cup peas - frozen or boiled
10-12 french beans - cut into small slanting pieces
1 carrot - cut into small cubes
1 capsicum - cut into small cubes
3-4 tbsp oil
1 tsp salt
½ tsp red chilli pd.
10-12 kaju (cashew nuts)
15-20 kishmish (raisins) - soaked in ½ cup water for 10 minutes
¼ cup (50 gms) fresh malai or cream
4-5 saboot kali mirch (pepper corns) - crushed to a powder

Kadhai Mushroom : page 42

1. Heat oil. Add onion rings & cook till they turn brown. Reduce flame.
2. Add kajus. Stir fry for 2-3 minutes.
3. Add beans & carrots. Cook covered till vegetables are done. Sprinkle 2-3 tbsp water occasionally if required.
4. Add capsicum & peas. Cook uncovered for another 3-4 minutes on low flame.
5. Add salt & red chilli powder to taste.
6. Add kishmish. Mix well for 1-2 minutes.
7. Add cream and crushed pepper corns. Mix. Remove from fire. Serve.

Mughlai Dum Aloo : page 24

ALOO TAMATAR SHOLA
Serves 4

4 small sized potatoes - peeled & cut into 1" pieces
5 tbsp dahi
3/4 tsp garam masala
1 tsp red chilli powder
1 tsp salt or to taste
5 tbsp oil
2 large onions - chopped
1" piece ginger - crushed to a paste
5-6 flakes garlic - crushed to a paste
5-7 almonds - powdered
1 tsp khus khus (poppy seeds)
1 tsp dessicated coconut
3 laung (cloves) - crushed
seeds of 2 moti illaichi (brown cardamoms) - crushed
2 sticks dalchini (cinnamon)

3-4 saboot kali mirch (black peppercorns)
½ cup water
1 tomato - cut into 8 pieces
2 tbsp chopped fresh coriander
2 green chillies - chopped

1. Beat dahi till smooth. Add garam masala & chilli powder. Keep aside.
2. Heat the oil and fry the onions until golden brown.
3. Add powdered almonds, khus khus, dessicated coconut, laung, moti illaichi, dalchini & kali mirch. Cook on low flame for 1 min.
4. Add ginger - garlic paste & salt. Cook for ½ minute.
5. Add dahi & blend it well. Stir-fry for about 2 minutes.
6. Stir in the potatoes. Cook for 2-3 minutes on low flame.
7. Add water, cover and simmer for 10-12 minutes or until the potatoes feel soft & are well cooked. Sprinkle a few tbsp water if required. Remove from fire.
8. At serving time, add tomatoes, fresh coriander and green chillies. Simmer for 2-3 minutes and serve immediately.

HARYALI KOFTA

Picture on inside front cover

Serves 6

KOFTA

150 gm paneer - crumbled
250 gm paalak (spinach)
½ tsp salt, ¼ tsp red chilli powder
1 tbsp cornflour
2 slices bread - dipped in water & squeezed

GRAVY

½ kg palak (spinach) - chopped
2 onions
1" piece ginger, 3-4 flakes garlic
2 tomatoes - chopped
¾ cup milk
½ tsp red chilli powder., ½ tsp salt or to taste, ¼ tsp pepper
3 tbsp oil, 1 tbsp ghee

1. To prepare koftas, remove stems of paalak leaves. Wash in plenty of water & pressure cook with ¼ cup water. Remove after the first whistle. Chop boiled paalak finely. Keep in a strainer for 10 minutes. Squeeze well. Mix paalak, paneer, bread, cornflour, red chilli powder and salt. Make balls. Roll in maida and deep fry.
2. To prepare the gravy, pressure cook ½ kg paalak with ½ cup water to give one whistle. Keep on low flame for 4-5 minutes. Blend to a paste in a grinder.
3. Blend the onions to a separate paste in a grinder.
4. Grind ginger & garlic to a paste. Blend tomatoes to a puree.
5. Heat 3 tbsp oil. Add onion paste and stir fry till golden brown.
6. Add tomatoes. Cook till dry. Add chilli powder & ginger-garlic paste. Cook on low flame for 5-7 minutes till tomatoes look well fried and oil separates. Remove from fire. Add milk, stirring constantly. Stir on low heat till dry.
7. Add paalak. Add salt & pepper. Stir fry for 5-7 minutes till paalak looks well fried and turns thick. Add ghee. Remove from fire.
8. Add koftas at the time of serving and heat for 1-2 minutes.

NUGGET MASALA
Serves 6

1 cup nutri nugget granules
1 cup milk
3 onions - chopped finely
8-10 flakes garlic - chopped & crushed
2 tomatoes - chopped finely
2 green chillies - chopped finely
1 cup boiled peas
3-4 laung (cloves) - crushed
1 tej patta (bay leaf)
5 tbsp oil
½ tsp garam masala
½ tsp red chilli pd.
1½ tsp salt or to taste
1" piece ginger - grated

1. Mix 1 cup milk & 1 cup water together. Boil. Add nutri nuggets. Soak for 15-20 minutes or more.
2. Heat 5 tbsp oil. Add onions. Cook till light brown. Add garlic. Cook for ½ minute.
3. Add tej patta, red chilli pd. and garam masala. Cook for ½ minute.
4. Add tomatoes & stir fry for 5-7 minutes on low flame.
5. Add soaked nutri nuggets. Stir fry till dry. Cook for 5-7 minutes more, till the nuggets are well fried.
6. Add boiled peas & salt. Stir fry for 2-3 minutes.
7. Add green chillies, grated or shredded ginger & crushed laung. Sprinkle some more garam masala, if desired. Stir fry for 2 minutes on low flame. Serve.

MASALEDAAR CHANNE KI DAL
Serves 4

1 cup channe ki dal - soaked for ½ hour
2 onions - chopped finely
1" piece ginger - chopped & crushed
6-8 flakes garlic - chopped & crushed
½ tsp red chilli pd
1 tsp dhania (coriander) powder
2 green chillies - slit lengthways
2 tomatoes chopped finely
3 tbsp ghee
½ tsp garam masala
2 tbsp chopped coriander
½ tsp haldi
salt to taste

1. Heat ghee in a pressure cooker. Add onions, cook till light brown.
2. Chop garlic & ginger. Crush on a chakla-belan. Add ginger-garlic paste to onions. Cook for ½ minute.
3. Add dhania pd. & ½ tsp red chilli powder. Cook for ½ minute.
4. Add tomatoes. Stir fry for 4-5 minutes till oil separates.
5. Add dal, haldi & green chillies. Fry for 5-7 minutes on low flame.
6. Add 2 cups water and salt. Pressure cook to give one whistle. After the first whistle, keep on low flame for 15 minutes.
7. At serving time, sprinkle chopped coriander and garam masala.

Note : The dal should not be watery. It should be quite thick.

PAALAK PANEER
Serves 6

½ kg paalak (spinach)
2 onions
1" piece ginger
2 green chillies
3-4 flakes garlic - optional
3 tomatoes - pureed or grated
crushed seeds of 2 moti illaichi (brown cardamom)
¼ tsp black pepper
salt to taste
4 tbsp ghee
200 gms paneer (cottage cheese) - cut into 1 " cubes

1. Chop paalak leaves, discarding the stalks. Wash in plenty of water. Pressure cook paalak with ¼ cup water to give one whistle. Keep on low flame for 10 minutes. Cool and blend in a mixer.
2. Grind onions, ginger, chillies & garlic together to a paste.
3. Grind tomatoes separately in a mixer or grate them.
4. Heat ghee. Add onion paste & cook till golden brown.
5. Add tomatoes. Cook till ghee separates.
6. Add spinach and cook for 10-15 minutes on low flame.
7. Add salt, moti illaichi and pepper. Remove from fire.
8. Cut paneer into 1" cubes, leaving aside some for garnishing. Deep fry to a golden colour.
9. Mix paneer pieces in the cooked spinach. Give it one boil.
10. Serve, garnished with finely grated paneer.

PESHAWARI BHEIN

Picture on page 18
Serves 4

250 gm bhein or kamal kakri (lotus stem) - (thick)
1 " piece ginger
4-5 flakes garlic
2 green chillies
½ tsp ajwain (thymol seeds)
1 tsp lemon juice
1 tbsp curd
3/4 tsp salt
½ tsp red chilli pd.
5-6 tbsp oil
2 tbsp atta (wheat flour)

1. Choose thick lotus stem (bhein). Cut bhein diagonally into ½ " thick, slanting pieces. Wash well. Use a toothpick to clean if it is dirty. Boil

in salted water till soft; or pressure cook in 1 cup water to give one whistle. Keep on low flame for 8-10 minutes.

2. Grind ginger, garlic, green chillies and ajwain to a paste.
3. Add lemon juice, curd, salt & red chilli pd. to the above paste. Mix well.
4. Strain the boiled bhein. Dry them. Apply the paste all over on the bhein. Keep aside for 1 hour.
5. At serving time, heat 5-6 tbsp oil. Reduce flame. Add atta. Cook for ½ - 1 minute till the atta turns golden brown.
6. Add the marinated (rubbed with paste) bhein & stir fry for 5-6 minutes on low flame till the atta coats the bhein.
7. Sprinkle some amchoor powder & garam masala. Stir fry for 2-3 minutes till they turn dry & crisp. Serve.

Note : • At the time of buying bhein, see that both the ends are closed. The closed ends prevent the dirt from going inside.
 • Do not buy very thin bhein.

HARE CHANNE KA SAALAN

Serves 6

FLAVOURING PASTE
1 tbsp khus khus (poppy seeds)
3 chhoti illaichi (green cardamom)
2" piece dry coconut or 1 tbsp dessicated (powder) coconut
3-4 laung (cloves)
1 tej patta
1 flower javitri (mace)
½ tbsp oil

OTHER INGREDIENTS
3 onions
½ " piece ginger
2 tomatoes
2 tsp dhania (coriander) powder
1½ cups hare channe or chholia (fresh green gram)

5-6 pieces of nutri nuggets - soaked in hot milk for 1 hour - optional
½ cup dahi - well beaten
1½ tsp salt or to taste
1 tsp red chilli powder
½ tsp garam masala
4 tbsp oil

1. To prepare the flavouring paste, collect together - khus khus, chhoti illaichi, dry coconut, laung, tej patta & javitri.
2. Heat ½ tbsp oil in a small heavy bottomed pan or on a tawa. Reduce flame. Add the collected spices together & fry on very low flame till khus khus turns golden. Remove tej patta.
3. Grind fried spices together to a rich aromatic paste. Keep paste aside.
4. Grind onions, tomatoes and ginger to a paste in a blender.
5. Heat 4 tbsp oil. Add dhania powder. Cook for ½ minute.
   Add the onion-tomato paste. Cook till oil separates. Reduce flame.
6. Add garam masala, red chilli powder & salt. Cook for ½ minute.

7. Beat curd with a fork & add to the onion masala. Cook, stirring till the masala turns brown again & oil separates.
8. Add the left over milk of the nutri nuggets. Cook till dry.
9. Add washed hare channe and the soaked nutri nuggets. Cook on low flame for 4-5 minutes.
10. Add 2 cups water. Boil. Cook on low flame till the hara channas get cooked.
11. Add the flavouring paste to the hare channe ki subzi.
12. Cover & keep on low flame for 5 minutes. Serve hot.

Zafrani Biryani : page 94

HANDI KATHAL
Serves 6

½ kg kathal (jackfruit)
4 onions - ground to a paste
½ pod garlic
2" piece ginger
2 tsp dhania (coriander) powder
1 tsp chilli pd.
¼ tsp haldi
1 stick dalchini (cinnamon)
4-5 laung (cloves) - crushed
3 tomatoes   chopped
½ cup dahi - beaten with a fork
salt to taste
¼ tsp garam masala

Subz Shahjhani : page 13

1. To keep the kathal from sticking to your hands, rub oil on your hands.
2. Remove the outer skin of the jackfruit with a sharp oiled knife. Cut into thick, big pieces, taking care that the pieces do not open up on cutting.
3. Deep fry the pieces to a golden brown colour & keep aside.
4. Grind onions to a paste in a blender.
5. Grind ginger & garlic to a separate paste.
6. Heat 6 tbsp oil. Add dhania powder. Cook for ½ minute on low flame. Add the onion paste & cook till light brown.
7. Add dalchini & crushed laung. Cook for ½ minute.
8. Add ginger - garlic paste. Cook for 1 minute on low flame. Add haldi & red chilli pd.
9. Add chopped tomatoes. Cook for 7-8 minutes, till tomatoes get mashed & the oil separates.
10. Add curd gradually and cook till masala turns brown again & oil separates.
11. Add salt and garam masala. Add 1 cup water. Boil.

12. Add the fried kathal pieces & cook covered on low flame for a few minutes, stirring very gently. Serve hot.

Note : • The kathal can be cut by the vegetable seller. It then becomes very simple to prepare this dish.
   • See that the kathal pieces remain intact in the masala. Do not stir too much, while heating.

ALOO PASANDA
Serves 6

2 large round potatoes
3 tbsp maida
4 tbsp water
¼ tsp salt
¼ tsp red chilli powder

FILLING
100 gms paneer - grated
8-10 kishmish - soaked in water & chopped
5-6 kaju - chopped
¼ tsp salt
a pinch of red chilli powder
a pinch of pepper

GRAVY
3 onions

3 tomatoes
1" piece ginger
5-6 flakes garlic
1 dry red chilli
4 tbsp oil
2 tej patta (bay leaf)
2-3 laung (cloves)
½ tsp red chilli pd.
1½ tsp dhania (coriander) powder
¼ tsp haldi
1½ tsp salt or to taste
2 tsp chilli-garlic tomato sauce

1. Peel potatoes. Wash & cut into very thin, round slices. Keep aside in salted water.
2. Mix grated paneer with all the ingredients of the filling lightly with a spoon. Do not mash the paneer.
3. Prepare a thick paste with 3 tbsp maida and 4 tbsp water to get a thick

batter of coating consistency. Add salt and red chilli pd.

4. Sandwich 1 tsp of filling between 2 slices of potato. Press well.
5. Heat oil for deep frying.
6. Dip, first the sides of the sandwiched potato slices in the maida batter & then the whole piece in the batter. Deep fry on low flame to a golden colour. See that the potatoes get cooked on frying. Keep aside.
7. To prepare the gravy, grind the onions, ginger, garlic, tomatoes and dry red chillies to a paste in a blender.
8. Heat 4 tbsp oil. Add onion-tomato paste. Add tej patta. Cook till paste turns dry.
9. Add haldi, dhania and red chilli powder. Add laung. Cook on low flame for 2-3 minutes till oil separates.
10. Add 1½ cups water. Boil. Add salt & tomato sauce. Simmer on low flame for 5-7 minutes. Keep aside.
11. At serving time, heat the gravy. Gently add the fried, stuffed aloos. Simmer for a minute. Garnish with chopped coriander & paneer grated directly on the vegetable in the dish.

ARBI NOORJAHANI
Serves 4

½ kg arbi (calocassia)
½ tsp ajwain (thymol seeds)
2 tbsp dhania (coriander) powder
1 tbsp amchoor (dried mango powder)
¼ cup chopped coriander
2 green chillies - cut into long strips
salt to taste, 1 tsp red chilli pd.

1. Pressure cook arbi with 3 cups water to give one whistle. Keep on low flame for 4-5 min. Do not over boil. Peel & flatten each piece between the palms. Heat 2 cups oil in a kadhai. Put 6-7 pieces of flattened arbi at one time in oil. Fry till golden. Remove from oil.

2. Heat ½ tbsp oil in a clean kadhai. Reduce flame. Add ajwain. Cook for ½ minute. Add dhania powder. Cook for ½ minute.

3. Add chilli powder, amchoor, salt, hara dhania & green chillies. Add 2-3 tbsp water. Add fried arbi. Stir fry for 1-2 minutes. Serve.

BHUTTA KACHUMAR
Serves 4

4 bhutte (corn on the cob)
1 cup milk
4 tbsp oil
2 onions - chopped finely
1 tej patta (bay leaf), 1 moti illaichi (brown cardamom)
¼ tsp haldi, 3/4 tsp salt or to taste
1 firm tomato - finely chopped, 1-2 tbsp chopped coriander

1. Grate 3 bhuttas on the grater. Remove whole corns from one bhutta by scraping with a knife. Pressure cook milk & corn together to give one whistle. Keep on low flame for 5 minutes.
2. Heat oil. Add onions, tej patta & crushed seeds of moti illaichi. Cook till onions turn transparent. Add haldi. Cook for ½ minute.
3. Add chopped tomato and cook for 3-4 minutes. Add corn & salt. Stir for 2-3 minutes. Mix coriander. Serve.

Mehfil-E-Kebab

RESHMI PANEER TIKKA
Serves 4-5

250 gms paneer - cut into ½ " thick, 1" squares

PASTE
1 tbsp curd
1½ " ginger piece
½ tsp jeera (cumin seeds)
3-4 flakes garlic - optional
2-3 dry, red, whole chillies
¼ tsp kala namak (rock salt)
a pinch of haldi
juice of ½ lemon
½ tsp salt

TO SERVE
4-5 tbsp thick cream or fresh malai

1 onion - cut into fine rings
3-4 tbsp chopped poodina (mint) leaves
1 tsp lemon juice

1. Grind ginger, jeera, garlic & red chillies to a fine paste.
2. Mix kala namak, haldi, curd, lemon juice & salt to the paste.
3. Rub this paste over the paneer pieces. Cover and keep aside for atleast 15 - 20 minutes or more, in the fridge.
4. At serving time, grill the paneer pieces by passing through skewers & keeping in a hot oven. Alternately, brown the paneer pieces in 2-3 tbsp oil in a non stick pan, on medium flame, turning carefully, to make both sides brown. Keep aside.
5. Heat malai or cream in a clean kadhai on very low flame, to make it just warm. Do not let it turn into ghee by keeping on the fire for a longer time.
6. Add the grilled paneer pieces. Toss gently.
7. Serve on a bed of onion rings sprinkled with chopped poodina & lemon juice.

POODINA DAL KEBABS
Serves 10-12

1½ cups channe ki dal
1 tsp salt
½ " piece ginger
4-5 flakes garlic
2½ cups water
4 slices bread
½ tsp garam masala (mixed spices)
½ tsp amchoor (dried mango pd.)
2-3 tbsp maida (plain flour) - to coat

FILLING
2-3 tbsp very finely chopped poodina
1 small onion - chopped finely
1 green chilli - chopped finely
¼ tsp amchoor
¼ tsp salt

1. Clean, wash dal. Pressure cook dal, salt, ginger, garlic & 2½ cups water together. After the first whistle, keep the cooker on low flame for 15 minutes.
2. Aftr the pressure drops down, mash the dal while it is hot, with a karchhi. Keep aside.
3. Dip bread slices in water for 1 second. Squeeze well to remove all the water. Add the squeezed bread, amchoor & garam masala to the boiled and mashed dal. Add salt to taste. Keep aside.
4. Mix all ingredients of the filling in a small bowl.
5. Make marble sized balls of the dal paste. Flatten them. Put ½ tsp of poodina mixture. Form a ball again. Flatten to form a kebab.
6. Roll in maida & deep fry 3-4 pieces at a time.
7. Serve hot with mint chutney.

GULNAR SEEKH KEBAB

Picture on cover
Makes 15

1 cup saboot masoor ki dal
1" piece ginger
8-10 flakes garlic
1 tsp jeera
1 tsp garam masala
1 tsp red chilli powder
3 slices bread - dipped in water & squeezed well
1 tsp salt or to taste
3 tbsp oil
2 tbsp each of finely chopped capsicum, onion & tomato (without pulp)

TO SERVE
2 onions - cut into rings
juice of 1 lemon
a few poodina leaves - finely chopped

1. Soak saboot masoor dal for 2 hours. Strain.
2. Grind dal, ginger, garlic and jeera to a thick paste using the minimum amount of water. Keep dal aside.
3. Heat 3 tbsp oil in a heavy bottomed kadhai. Add dal. Stir fry for 4-5 minutes on low flame till dal is dry and does not stick to the bottom of the kadhai.
4. Remove sides of bread & dip in water for a second. Squeeze well & crumble finely. Mix bread, salt, garam masala & red chilli powder with the dal. Mash well. Keep aside.
5. Heat 3-4 tbsp oil on a tawa or a nonstick pan for shallow frying.
6. Grease a pencil or a thick knitting needle. Spread a ball of dal paste along the length of the pencil, such that the pencil is inserted in the roll. Make a 2 " long kebab of the dal paste over the pencil or needle.
7. Stick finely chopped onion, capsicum & tomatoes (without pulp) on the kebab on the pencil, by pressing onions etc. with the palm on to the kebab. Gently pull out the pencil & shallow fry the seekh in medium hot oil to a light brown colour. Serve hot on a bed of onion rings sprinkled with lemon juice and chopped poodina leaves.

VEGETABLE KAJOO KEBAB
Makes 8-10

2 big potatoes - chopped
2 small onions - chopped
3/4 cup shelled peas
½ of a small cauliflower - cut into small florets
1 " piece ginger - crushed
5-6 flakes garlic - crushed
1 green chilli - finely chopped
½ tsp red chilli powder
½ tsp garam masala
2 tsp tomato sauce
1½ tsp salt or to taste
2 tbsp chopped fresh coriander
10 -12 cashewnuts - finely chopped
2 bread slices - sides removed & mashed (crumbled)
OR
4 tbsp bread crumbs

1. Pressure cook potatoes, cauliflower, onion & peas with 1 cup water to give one whistle. Drain and leave in a sieve for about 5 minutes to remove excess moisture.
2. Mash the vegetables and add ginger, garlic, red chilli pd, garam masala, salt and tomato sauce. Add the fresh coriander & bread.
3. Mix in the cashewnuts. Break off small balls of the vegetable mixture and pat them into flat circular shapes about ½ " thick, with the palms of your hands.
4. Heat 4-5 tbsp oil in a frying pan or on a tawa and fry gently over medium heat, turning once.
5. Remove on a kitchen towel to remove excess oil.

VEGETARIAN SHAMI KEBAB
Serves 8

½ cup kale channe (black gram)
1 tbsp channe ki dal (bengal gram split)
3-4 laung (cloves)
3-4 saboot kali mirch (pepper corns)
½ " piece ginger - chopped
1 dry red chilli
2 slices bread - dipped in water & squeezed
salt to taste
½ tsp amchoor (dried mango pd.)

FILLING
1 tbsp chopped coriander
1 tsp khus khus (poppy seeds)
1 onion - very finely chopped
½ " piece ginger - grated finely

1 green chilli - chopped very finely
salt to taste

1. Soak kale channe with channe ki dal overnight or for 6-8 hours in 2 cups of water.
2. Pressure cook kale channe, channe ki dal, laung, saboot kali mirch, ginger and red chilli together. After the first whistle, keep on slow fire for 20 minutes.
3. If there is extra water, dry the channe for sometime on fire. There should just be a little water, enough to grind the channas to a fine paste.
4. Grind to a fine paste. Add soaked bread, salt, red chilli powder and amchoor to taste.
5. Mix all ingredients of the filling together.
6. Make a small ball of the paste. Flatten it, put 1 tsp of filling and make a ball again. Flatten it slightly.
7. Deep fry 4-5 pieces in medium hot oil. Serve.

KATHAL KEBAB
Makes 15

½ kg kathal (jackfruit)
1" piece ginger, 10-12 flakes garlic
½ tsp jeera (cumin seeds)
2 dry red chillies
2 tbsp besan (gram flour)
1tsp garam masala, ½ tsp amchoor, salt to taste
4 tbsp bread crumbs - sifted

1. Cut jackfruit into big pieces by rubbing oil on your hands as well as on the knife. Pressure cook with 1 cup water to give one whistle. Keep on low flame for 5 minutes. Strain. Remove seeds.
2. Blend kathal, ginger, garlic, jeera & red chillies to a fine paste without any water. Mix 1 tbsp besan with the kathal paste. Mix chilli powder, garam masala, sifted bread crumbs & salt to taste.
3. Make balls with greased or wet hands. Flatten. Shallow fry on a tawa or pan till brown. Serve.

Nazaakat-E-Biryani

ZAFRANI BIRYANI

Picture on page 71
Serves 4

1cup basmati rice
3-4 chhoti illaichi (green cardamoms) - crushed
2 tej patta (bay leaves)
2 laung (cloves)
1 tsp butter or desi ghee
2½ tsp salt
juice of ½ lemon
8 cups water

VEGETABLE LAYER
10 - 12 french beans - cut into tiny cubes
2 carrots - cut into tiny cubes
½ cup boiled or frozen peas
2 tbsp butter or ghee

2 tbsp curd
½ tsp garam masala
½ " piece ginger - crushed to a paste
½ tsp red chilli pd
3/4 tsp salt

OTHER INGREDIENTS
4 onions - sliced & deep fried
2 tbsp milk
few strands of kesar (saffron)
8-10 kaju - fried

1. Clean, wash & soak rice for 15 minutes.
2. Boil plenty of water (8 cups approx.) in a large pan. Add chhoti illaichi, tej patta, laung, salt, desi ghee or butter & lemon juice.
3. Drain soaked rice & add to the boiling water. Boil till rice is just done. See that the rice is not over cooked. It may be slightly under cooked but certainly not over cooked.

4. Strain the rice. Keep aside.
5. Cut beans & carrots into small cubes.
6. Heat butter in a clean kadhai. Add beans & carrots. Cook, covered on low flame till done. Add peas.
7. Add garam masala, salt & red chilli pd.
8. Crush ginger on a chakla-belan. Blend curd with crushed ginger. Mix curd with the vegetables. Stir fry for 3 minutes. Keep vegetables aside.
9. Deep fry the sliced onions in a heavy bottomed kadhai, to a golden brown colour and keep aside.
10. Soak kesar in warm milk for 10 - 15 minutes.
11. To assemble the biryani, grease an oven proof dish with butter or ghee.
12. Put half of the rice. Spread evenly with a fork.
13. Spread half of the cooked vegetables over the rice.
14. Spread a layer of fried onions using half the onions.
15. Spread the left over rice over the onions.
16. Spread the vegetables over the rice.

17. Put the left over onions on the vegetables.
18. Rub the kesar strands to extract the flavour & colour. Sprinkle kesar along with the milk over the fried onions.
19. Garnish with fried kaju. Cover with foil & keep aside.
20. To serve, keep in a moderately hot oven for 10 minutes.

Note : • Fry onions in a heavy bottomed kadhai for even browning.
   • Boil rice in a large pan. Do not overcook the rice.
   • Do not heat the oven too much.

ALOO MATAR KI TAHARI
Serves 4

1 cup basmati rice - soaked for 1 hour
1 medium onion - sliced finely
2 tbsp ghee or unsalted butter
1 tej patta (bay leaves)
½ " piece ginger - crushed
¼ tsp haldi
1 small potato - cut into round slices
1 cup shelled peas
2 cups water
1 tbsp chopped coriander
1½ tsp salt or to taste

1. Soak rice for 1 hour
2. Fry the sliced onion in the ghee or butter until golden brown.
3. Add tej patta, ginger & haldi. Cook for 1 minute.
4. Add the potatoes and peas and stir-fry over low heat for about 2-3 minutes.
5. Add the drained rice and mix everything together.
6. Add the water and fresh coriander & salt. Boil. Lower the temperature and cook covered, for 12-15 minutes or until the rice is done.
7. Serve hot with a refreshing raita.

METHI TAMATAR PULLAO
Serves 4

1 cup basmati rice - soaked for 1 hour
4 tbsp oil
2 tbsp kasoori methi (dried fenugreek leaves)
½ tsp jeera (cumin seeds)
1½ tsp salt
3 medium tomatoes - chopped finely
2 cups water

1. Soak rice for 1 hour.
   Heat oil in a saucepan. Reduce flame. Add jeera. Fry for about ½ minute till jeera turns golden.
2. Add chopped tomatoes and stir everything together. Continue to fry for about 5-7 minutes, mashing the tomatoes well. Continue to stir fry till oil separates.
3. Add kasoori methi. Stir fry for 1 minute.
4. Add the rice and stir everything well.
5. Add water, stir once more and cover the saucepan. Boil. Reduce heat and simmer the rice for about 12-15 minutes, or until the rice is cooked.
6. Allow to stand for about 5-7 minutes, and serve hot.

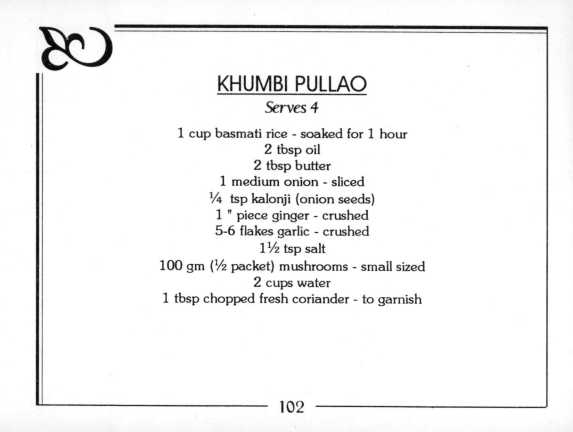

KHUMBI PULLAO
Serves 4

1 cup basmati rice - soaked for 1 hour
2 tbsp oil
2 tbsp butter
1 medium onion - sliced
¼ tsp kalonji (onion seeds)
1 " piece ginger - crushed
5-6 flakes garlic - crushed
1½ tsp salt
100 gm (½ packet) mushrooms - small sized
2 cups water
1 tbsp chopped fresh coriander - to garnish

1. Soak rice for 1 hour.
2. Heat oil and butter in a heavy bottomed pan. Add kalonji. Cook for ½ minute.
3. Add onions and fry the onions until light brown.
4. Add ginger, garlic and salt. Cook for 1 minute on low flame.
5. Add the whole mushrooms and stir-fry for about 2 minutes.
6. Drain the rice and add the rice and stir gently for ½ minute.
7. Add water. Boil, lower the heat, cover and simmer for 12-15 minutes or until the water has been absorbed and the rice is cooked.
8. Leave to stand for 5-7 minutes to allow the rice to dry out a little.
9. Serve garnished with fresh coriander.

Note : If mushrooms are big, cut them into halves.

MILONI TAHARI
Serves 6

1½ cups basmati rice - soaked for 1 hour
10 french beans - cut into 1" diagonal pieces
1 small carrot - cut into slanting slices
¼ of a small cauliflower
1 small potato - cut into four big pieces
1 onion
2 tomato
1" ginger piece
5-6 flakes garlic
2 laung (cloves)
1 stick dalchini (cinnamon)
1 tsp garam masala
2 tsp salt
1 tsp lemon juice
5-6 tbsp oil

1. Soak rice for **1 hour**.
2. Grind onion, tomatoes, ginger, and garlic to a paste in a mixer.
3. Cut all vegetables into big pieces. Cut beans and carrots diagonally
4. Heat oil in a heavy bottomed pan. Add the onion-tomato paste. Cook till dry.
5. Add laung & dalchini.
6. Add the vegetables. Cook for 5-7 minutes, till oil separates and the masala is dry.
7. Drain the soaked rice & add to the vegetables. Mix well.
8. Add garam masala & salt. Mix.
9. Add 3 cups (double the amount of rice) water. Add lemon juice. Boil. Cover and cook on low flame till rice is done. Serve after 10 minutes.

SUBZ BIRYANI
Serves 5-6

PASTE
6-7 flakes garlic
1" piece ginger
1 tbsp saunf (aniseeds)
1 tsp jeera (cumin seeds)
3 red chillies
1 tsp dhania (coriander) powder
1 stick dalchini (cinnamon)
3-4 laung (cloves)
3-4 saboot kali mirch (pepper corns)
seeds of 2 moti illaichi (brown cardamom)

OTHER INGREDIENTS
2 cups basmati rice - soaked for 1 hour
1-2 carrots - cut diagonally into slices

1 small cauliflower - cut into big floretes
8-10 french beans - cut into 1" long diagonal pieces
2 small potatoes - cut into fours
2 onions - sliced finely
½ cup oil
3 tsp salt
1 tsp lemon juice
1 tej patta (bay leaf)

1. Soak rice for 1 hour.
2. Grind the ingredients of the paste together with a little water.
3. Heat oil in a heavy bottomed pan. Add onions, cook till golden brown.
4. Add the vegetables and stir fry for 3-4 minutes.
5. Add the paste and tej patta.
6. Measure 4 cups of water and add to the vegetables.
7. Add salt & lemon juice.
8. When water boils, drain the soaked rice and add to the water.

9. Put a tawa under the pan of rice to reduce the heat further.
10. Cover the pan of rice with a small towel napkin and then with a well fitting lid. Keep some heavy weight, on the lid.
11. Slow down the fire and cook till the rice is done (10-15 minutes).
12. Serve after 10 minutes.

Daawat-E-Rotiyan

LACHHA PARANTHA
Makes 6

2 cups atta (wheat flour)
½ tsp salt
½ cup milk
½ cup water
2 tbsp ghee

1. Sift the flour and salt together in a paraat (deep bowl).
2. Mix water & milk together in a cup.
3. Make a well in the middle & pour the milk & water mixture gradually. Mix and knead to form a dough of rolling consistency.
4. Knead some more. Keep aside, covered for ½ an hour.
5. Make 6 balls. Roll out each ball to a circle of 6" diameter.
6. Spread some ghee all over.
7. Sprinkle dry atta on half of the circle. Fold into half to get a semi circle.

8. Spread ghee all over again. Put dry atta on half part of the semi circle. Fold again into half so that you get a long strip.
9. Apply ghee all over on the strip. Roll the strip from one end till the end, to form a flattened ball (pedha).
10. Press gently. Roll out, applying very little pressure, to form the lachha parantha. If pressure is applied, the layers stick to each other and do not open up on frying.
11. Stick in a heated tandoor or shallow fry on a tawa. Place on a clean napkin & crush the parantha slightly, to open up the layers. Serve hot.

NAN BADAAMI

Picture on page 18
Makes 6

2½ cups (250 gms) maida (plain flour)
½ cup hot milk
½ tsp baking powder
½ cup warm water (approx)
½ tsp salt
10 badaam (almonds) - skinned & cut into long thin pieces

NAN AFGHANI

This nan is prepared with atta (whole wheat flour). The dough is prepared with half maida (1¼ cups) & half atta (1¼ cups). The rest of the ingredients and the method are the same as for baadami nan. No almonds are put on the nan.

1. Heat milk and put it in a paraat (large pan). Add baking powder to the hot milk. Mix well and keep it aside for 1-2 minutes.
2. Sift maida & salt together. Add maida to the hot milk. Mix.
3. Knead to a dough with enough warm water.
4. Keep in a warm place for 3-4 hours.
5. Make 6-8 balls.
6. Roll out each ball to an oblong shape. Spread ghee all over. Fold one side (lengthways) a little, so as to overlap an inch of the nan. Press on the joint with the belan (rolling pin).
7. Sprinkle some blanched (skin removed by dipping in hot water) almonds. Press with a rolling pin (belan). Pull one side of the nan to give it a pointed end like the shape of the nan.
8. Apply some water on the back side of the nan. Stick in a hot tandoor.
9. Cook till nan is ready. Spread butter on the ready nan and serve hot.

POODINA PARANTHA
Makes 6

2 cups atta (whole wheat flour)
4 tbsp freshly chopped or dry poodina (mint leaves)
1 tsp ajwain (thymol seeds)
2 tbsp oil
½ tsp salt
½ tsp red chilli powder

1. Mix atta with all ingredients except poodina. Add enough water to make a dough of rolling consistency.
2. Make walnut sized balls. Flatten to make a thick chappati.
3. Spread 1 tsp of ghee all over. Cut a slit from the outer edge till the centre. Start rolling from the slit to form a cone. Press cone gently
4. Roll out. Sprinkle poodina. Press with the belan (rolling pin).
5. Cook on a tawa, frying on both sides or apply some water on the back side of the parantha and stick it in a hot tandoor.

MISSI ROTI

Picture on inside front cover
Makes 6

1 cup besan (gram flour)
1 cup atta (whole wheat flour)
2 tbsp oil or melted ghee
1 tbsp kasoori methi (dry fenugreek leaves)
½ tsp salt, ½ tsp red chilli powder
½ tsp jeera (cumin seeds)
a pinch of hing (asafoetida)
a pinch of haldi (turmeric powder)

1. Mix all ingredients. Add enough water to make a dough of rolling consistency. Cover it and keep aside for ½ hour.
2. Make 6 balls. Roll each ball into a chappati, but slightly thick.
3. Cook on a hot tawa by frying it or in a hot tandoor.
4. When made in a tandoor, apply ghee and serve immediately.

LAZEEZ KULCHE
Makes 8

DOUGH

250 gms (2½ cups) maida (plain flour)
¼ tsp dry yeast
¼ tsp baking powder
150 ml (1 cup) warm milk
1 tsp salt, 1 tsp sugar
1½ tsp oil
1 tbsp curd

FILLING

1 small bunch of poodina (mint) leaves
3/4 tsp ajwain (thymol seeds)
3/4 tsp salt
3/4 tsp red chilli pd.
1 big onion - very finely chopped
2 tbsp chopped coriander leaves

1. Dissolve yeast in 2-3 tbsp of warm water.
2. Sift maida. Add sugar and salt.
3. Put curd in the centre of the maida and sprinkle baking powder on it. Leave for a few seconds till it starts bubbling.
4. Add oil and the dissolved yeast. Knead with warm milk to a dough. The dough should neither be too soft nor too stiff. It becomes loose after it is kept away for a few hours.
5. Grease a polythene, brush the dough with oil. Keep the dough in the polythene, cover it with a pan inverted over it. Keep in the sun or a warm place for 3-4 hours.
6. The dough swells. Knead it again. Keep aside.
7. Make balls. Roll out to the desired size. Sprinkle filling all over.
8. Press gently with the rolling pin (belan) and then with your fingers.
9. Stick in a heated tandoor by applying water on the back side of the kulcha.
10. Cook till brown spots appear. Serve hot.

<u>MOOLI PARANTHA</u>
Makes 6

2 cups atta (wheat flour)
2 tbsp ghee
½ tsp salt

FILLING
2 big moolis (radish)
½ tsp ajwain (thymol seeds)
1½ tsp salt
½ tsp red chilli pd
tender leaves of one mooli
a pinch of amchoor (dried mango pd.)
½ tsp garam masala

1. Knead atta and salt together with enough water to form a dough of rolling consistency. Cover & keep aside.
2. Grate moolis. Finely chop a few leaves very finely & mix with the grated mooli. Add salt & keep aside for 15 minutes.
3. Squeeze the grated mooli in small batches to remove the water.
4. Mix ajwain, red chilli pd & amchoor. Add garam masala.
5. Make marble sized balls of the dough. Roll 2 balls into 2 thin chappatis.
6. Spread 2-3 tbsp of the filling all over one chappati & cover with the second chappati to make one stuffed parantha. Press the edges to seal.
7. Sprinkle a little flour on the stuffed parantha & roll out lightly.
8. Fry on a hot tawa, putting ghee from the sides, to make the edges crisp.
9. Serve hot with plain dahi.

NITA MEHTA'S BEST SELLING TITLES BY
COOKERY BOOKS

1. All-time favourite SNACKS* **
2. Best of CHINESE Vegetarian Cuisine* **
3. Breakfast & Brunch (Non Veg)
4. Breakfast Special
5. Cakes & Chocolates*
6. CHINESE Cooking for the Indian Kitchen
7. CHINESE Non Veg
8. Chutneys Squashes Pickles
9. Corn and Pasta
10. Dal & Roti* ***
11. Delicious Parlour ICE CREAMS
12. Desserts & Puddings* **
13. Different Ways with CHAAWAL**
14. Favourite Non Vegetarian Dishes
15. Flavours of INDIAN COOKING
16. Green Vegetables
17. Handi Tawa Kadhai
18. Healthy & Delicious FOOD FOR CHILDREN
19. Indian Vegetarian Cookbook (Paperback)
20. JHATPAT KHAANA-Vegetarian
21. Low Calorie Desserts

22. LOW CALORIE RECIPES Non Veg
23. Low Calorie Recipes**
24. MICROWAVE Non Veg Cookery
25. MICROWAVE Vegetarian Cookery* **
26. More PANEER
27. MUGHLAI Vegetarian Khaana*
28. NAVRATRI Special Recipes
29. PANEER All the Way* ** ***
30. Perfect Vegetarian Cookery (P.B)
31. SANDWICHES
32. SNACKS Non-Veg
33. Soups Salads & Starters
34. South Indian Favourites
35. Starters & Mocktails
36. Taste of KASHMIR
37. Taste of PUNJAB - Vegetarian
38. Taste of RAJASTHAN- Veg
39. The Art of BAKING
40. The Best of CHICKEN Recipes*
41. The Best of Vegetarian Dishes
42. Vegetarian Wonders (Paperback)

*Also available in Hindi, ** Also available in Gujarati, *** Also available in Bengali

For Details about *Nita Mehta* Cookery Books & Classes, Call: 6214011, 6238727 (DELHI)